D0723366

Howard, Richard,
1929-
Without saying

WITHOUT SAYING

RICHARD HOWARD

Without Saying

NEW POEMS

TURTLE POINT PRESS

NEW YORK

2008

ISBN 978-1-933527-14-7

LCCN 2007907229

Design and composition by
Wilsted & Taylor Publishing Services

The author thanks the editors of the following
publications, in which these poems first appeared:
Five Points: "The Rape of the Daughters of Leucippus
by Castor and Pollux"; *Guernica*: "Only Different";
New Republic: "School Days: ii. Arthur Englander's Back in
School"; *Parnassus*: "To Constantine Cavafy," "Family Secrets,"
"School Days: i. Back from Our Spring Trip"; *Salmagundi*:
"Notes of an Industrious Apprentice"; *Seattle Review*:
"Mind Under Matter"; *Tri-Quarterly*: "Exposures:
i. Taken for a Ride"; *Western Humanities Review*:
"School Days: iv. What the Future Has in Store"

FOR DAVID ALEXANDER

IT GOES

CONTENTS

WITHOUT SAYING

Only Different

FOR SEYMOUR KLEINBERG

WHO REMINDS ME WHAT

KATE CROY KNEW

I

HOTEL DEL CORONADO

MAY 2, 1904

Papa dearest, please
don't think for a moment I'm finding fault—
as things turned out, it was a piece of luck
you left behind those two "late" books of his
that Uncle Henry sent last year when you
were at Palo Alto lecturing on
Pragmatism and the Sense of Common Sense.
You'll soon see why we needed specimens
of Uncle's recent work (anything but
thick on the ground in this locale), and lo!
there they were in your old rooms at Stanford.

Bruce says it was Fate,
and I assure you
it never occurred to either of us
to attribute their preternatural
existence in the Far West (wild or tame)
to whether you *had* or *hadn't* read them.
The great thing is that books by Henry James
are *here*! And now for the explanation:
Poor Uncle complained—surely, Papa, you'll
recognize the tune—of being so "spent
by the myriad claims of nine hundred
members of a female culture club
                    in Los Angeles"
that with promises
of quiet and cuisine we conveyed him
to this hotel on Coronado Beach,
the grandest in the State—or in the States!—
where even Uncle could recuperate
or, in his words, "lie awake nights listening
to the languid lisp of the Pacific."
When the Manager showed us the Grand Suite
which had been reserved for Uncle's repose,

he further revealed, in reverent tones
befitting the Grandeur of it all, that
                    "another author,
quite a famous one,
occupies (with his wife and his five sons)
the matching rooms in the opposite wing,
a Mr. Baum—L. Frank Baum is the name
he uses," we were informed, "for his books,"
which books (there are but two so far) have won
a fervent audience of young readers
vast enough to constitute actual fame.
It's true—Bruce himself has given his niece
the Oz books—and it occurred to us
that after a fitting interval of
                    del Coronado
comforts, Uncle might
like to invite the young author to lunch
—he must be young to have those readers—
and I, meanwhile, would obtain the Oz books
to further ensure Uncle's taking part
in such regalement, convinced as I am
that after a regular regimen

of "900 cultured female members,"
Baum might afford Uncle some refreshment.
Bruce has already supplied that sort of
enkindling company for him, and is
                            now determined to
sound out Mr. Baum,
who might, for all we know, be a shy old
recluse reluctant to meet anyone
so august as Henry James. But five sons!
wouldn't any father enjoy some relief
from all that filial life? . . . We're leaving
Uncle here for a week (with the Oz books),
while I help Bruce pack, and then we all make
our ways back to Chocorua: despite
the lurid splendors of California
                            (Uncle claims they are
"solely vegetal:
Italy without the castles"), I miss
the shy glories of a New England spring;
I'm so glad Mother wants the wedding at
the Chocorua house—Bruce's parents say

they are thrilled to be visiting that part
of the country, and I'm sure you'll
love them as we love Bruce, who says he'll write
after our historic luncheon with
that famous author, Mr. L. Frank Baum.
                    Having actually
read *The Land of Oz*,
Bruce claims it would be madness to suppose
these two poles of American Romance
—does *What Maisie Knew* fit at the North Pole?
The Land of Oz at the South?—could even
hypothesize each other's existence . . .
He says by bringing them together we
might do our native literature some
service by making antipodean
extremities meet, or at least, *meet us*!
I send all my love, and Bruce would send his
                    if he were here,
                              Peg

HOTEL DEL CORONADO

MAY 7, 1904

Peggot, dearest niece,
what could you have hoped to effect, in terms
of collegial communion (if this was
your initial goal?) or even the mere
polite impingement of fellow-strangers
in this ever so richly cupola'd
and columniated caravansary,
by allowing—indeed by *exhorting*
your helplessly critical old uncle
to acquaint himself all too utterly
with the literary productions of
                    Mr. L. Frank Baum?
Any neophyte
with a sweet tooth sufficiently sharpened
by commercial enticement (I allude
thus indelicately, dear child, prompted
by eons of promiscuous exposure
to the twaddle of a tribe deluded

by the notion that to write for children
one need be merely childish), any scribbler
—and this *Tree* you set before me is
the unconditional epitome
of the dreadful forest I speak of—
                              might be counted on
to commit (indulged
by an infantile reading or *read-to*
public), and not merely to commit *one*
Book of Oz but quite incorruptibly
to deliver two already—and more
sequellae liable to disembogue
from such a source—a series infinite:
If *Wizard*, then why not Witch? If *Land*,
then as likely bring forth Sea, Sky, indeed
a veritable (*invraisemblable*)
                         Library of Oz!
Nonetheless, dear niece,
my Ozian? Ozite? Ozic? dismay
has left me neither deaf nor blind
to possibilities latent in one
Suggestive Scene occurring late, but for

my interest, in the nick of time in those
alas far from singular volumes
which you so culpably bestowed (if only
to dissipate my *ennui hôtelière*) . . .
It is the case that what your father has
habitually diagnosed as my
                  "compositional
scabies" was aroused,
only to be routed, by Baum's treatment
(or *lack* of treatment) of an episode
in the final chapters of . . . *The Land of Oz* . . .
What a betrayal it was to dissolve
the spell a "wicked witch" had cast upon
the one pleasing and the sole plausible
human being in the entire *galère*
of ghouls, goblins and gear-driven gadgets—
upon the boy hitherto known as Tip,
who by a highly inappropriate
                  if not scandalous
metamorphosis
(its real motive being to ready Baum's
unwary readers for the subsequent

installment of—*forgive me*—looming Ooze)
emerges from the Sorceress's cloud
of occult incense, numbly smiling at
his former companions' misgiving stares,
now emerges gorgeously gowned, girdled,
and garlanded by wanton peonies
gaudily arrayed (but how planted? how
plucked? how plaited together?)—as OZMA
                    lost Princess of Oz!
Now Peggot darling,
I still retain (however deep in my
dotage I may appear) a sufficient
compositional *astuce* to discern
the disastrous pointlessness of turning
Tip *back* into Ozma, without having
first shown the effects of the Princess's
consciousness she had become a Boy;
here we have a fable undertaking
to account for the composition of
true majesty, which as the ancients taught,
                    involves a double
royal gendering:

it's all well and good to secrete Ozma
from danger as the estimable Tip,
but somehow in the process she must know
herself *as him*, thereafter he *as her*;
instead of which important emblem of
royal self-consciousness, we're served a scene
of futile consolation offered to
the dismay of Tip's old friends, compounded
by the Princess's unimpressive lie
uttered in bland reproof: "I'm just the same
                    as I always was—
only different!"
How inescapably we learn we are
never just the same as we always were.
Didn't Kate Croy speak words to that effect?
Aside from his botched Transformation Scene,
Baum's narrative (I veil the sacred name:
the Oz books are *never* novels) might have been
run up by a seamstress overfond of sweets
who had eaten one too many *éclairs*
and slept upon her back to ill effect
before scribbling such a text, and one *so*

ill-illustrated—
though in that regard
I'm altogether unaware of what
poor Baum's responsibilities may be,
and wish to remain so. Indeed, dear Peg,
it's best that I remove myself from all
propinquity likely to result in
a meeting, however accidental
and nugatory, between the author,
as he must be called, of *The Land of Oz*
and your fond but (in the gift of this grand
hospice) firmly sequestered old
                                    Uncle

III

HOTEL CORONADO
MAY 11, 1904

Dear Associate,
you type your standing
at Stanford University beneath

your signature, so I assume that though
but an "associate," you are to be
addressed as *Professor Bruce Porter*
on more formal occasions than this note
in answer to yours (and its enclosure)
of last week. It was kind, I believe, and
generous as well that no sooner had
you found me at the Coronado than
you asked me to lunch with your fiancée
and, more to the point,

> your uncle-in-law

to-be who, it appears, is a famous
Man of Letters (unknown to me, although
something in your tone implied I might jump
at the chance to meet Mr. Henry James).
Well, I *have* lately corresponded with
one William James, who is, I now learn, his
brother and your future father-in-law.
It was, as I say, generous to send
one of that brother's books with your letter
—it was positively prescient! Do you,

> as I do, believe

in Second Sight, and
Other Worlds than this one? I have long since
accepted Theosophy's doctrines, and
rejoice that my wife Maud and I had met
in Earlier Incarnations . . . And like
William James, I too attend séances
in the hope of obtaining objective
evidence of the reality of spirits
and the afterlife. Unfortunately
I could not find in *Henry* James's book
a trace of the spiritual. Such writing
                        supports literature
like the rope that holds
a hanged man, and this book, *What Maisie Knew*,
seems merely an overheated hothouse,
perfumed but tainted, for in *this* James's
London society, transgressions of
the Few bear witness to depravities
of the Many. The novelist himself
has taken sick, and his toilsome language
creeps across the page, line after crapulous
line, like so many worms (though merely words!) . . .

Professor Porter, I have endeavored,
                          with my girls and boys,
to articulate
all that is healthy and, in every sense,
spirited in the Youth of our country;
had I taken poor Maisie as a sign
or (Lord help us!) a model, Dorothy
could never have survived a day in Oz,
for what is Oz but where we are, Magic
and all? . . . At the end, what Maisie knew is
what everyone else knows already: who
has money, who hasn't. It is *William* James
who tells the Truth: our American form
                          of fulfillment is
"worship of the bitch-
goddess success." That is our national
disease—yet all I find in his brother's
novel, in which he chews so much more
than he can bite off, is bitching about
the bush. No goddess even . . . Dear Porter,
having read thus far into my ill temper,
you will forgive me if I choose to skip

your luncheon-party, which will be no less
agreeable for the absence of one
guest, invited perhaps but, I am now
                    convinced, unwelcome.
Yours,
        Lyman Frank Baum

PA LO A LTO

MAY 1 5 , 1 9 0 4

                    Dear Professor James,
Peg and I supposed
that in the time between the End of Term
and our cross-country trip to New Hampshire
there might be a Cultural Adventure
in store for us: escorting your brother
to San Diego for a week's relief
from lecturing—from the *audiences*
he lectures to—we learned that L. Frank Baum,
author of a couple of fantastic

(and fantastically popular) books
for children, more or less, was living on
what Henry James calls
             the *lagniappe* of such
popularity in the same hotel;
perhaps it was the inordinateness
of the Del Coronado, a really
extravagant resort, which inspired
our scheme: we proposed to this pair of
antithetical literary lights
who, I was rightly sure, had never heard
of one another, that they have what their
various readers would nevertheless
view as a veritable "author's lunch."
                         (An inducement, or
at least a safety-net:
Peg would supply her Uncle with the two
Oz Books, while I would present Mr. Baum
with *Maisie* and *The Wings of the Dove*, still
in your old rooms at Stanford. Thus forearmed,
our two masters would know what sort of meal
they were in for.) . . . Well, by now I assume

Peg has written to describe our project's
total collapse: upon perusal of
each other's literature, *both* authors
declined our invitation to luncheon,
                              and I think it best
to protect you from
the terms of *either* repudiation
(I fear such withholding is a lot
like the riddle in one of HJ's tales).
On this occurrence the only "marriage
of true minds" will be the one between Peg's
and mine, concerning which the two of us
feel in the clear. Next week my parents and I
leave from San Francisco; Peg and HJ
meet up with us in Chicago to catch
the Twentieth Century Limited.
                              Symbolic enough?
With my affection,
                              Bruce

Pederasty

TO DANIEL HALÉVY

If I had money from a boundless mint
and sinew enough in hands, lips, loins,
I'd shun the vanity of politics and print,
and leave—tomorrow? no, *tonight!*—for lawns

luminous with artificial green
(*without* the rustic flaws of frost and vermin),
where I'd forever be sleeping with one
warm child or other: François? Firmin? . . .

For what is *manly mockery* to me?
Let Sodom's apples burn, acre by acre,
I'd savor still the sweat of those sweet limbs!

Beneath a solar gold, a lunar nacre,
I'd . . . *languish* (an *ars moriendi* of my own),
deaf to the knell of dreary Decency!

from the French of Marcel Proust (1888)

To Constantine Cavafy

AND FOR DANIEL MENDELSOHN,

INVOLUNTARY ACCOMPLICE

At twenty (implausible age, as we now
visualize you, but you *were* twenty once)
    you found in the *Revue des Deux Mondes*
    not even a reproduction but
        what must have impressed you as
    a stimulatingly detailed though
    somewhat disrespectful account
of Gustave Moreau's *Oedipus and the Sphinx*,
in its season the scandal of the Salon,
    and ever since a source of dismay.
    Yet you were moved to rehearse the tale
        in the all-too-plausible
    verses of your *juvenilia*,
    now consigned to the implacable
purgatory of "Rejected Poems."
Although this particular confrontation

(gorgeously limned the year you were born
by a young man who like you would live
        with his mother till she died)
    must have altogether seduced you
    as young Moreau envisioned it or
as you divined that vision from some ambitious
feuilleton merely describing it—nonetheless
        the fabled Heroic Encounter
        failed to lure you into its clutches
            ever again: there would be
        no future Cavafy transaction
        with this early Oedipal matter,
regardless of all the beautiful young men
(hardly heroes, though often in like undress)
        who took starring or supporting roles
        in your epic memory. But of course
            if you *had* seen the canvas
        (as I have: here in New York City
        where it enjoys—endures?—pride of place
in our great museum's Symbolist freak-show),
    minus the insolent elucidation
        of some hebdomadal hack, you might

have been motivated to produce
    canonical Cavafy
    rather than "rejected verse"—why not
    an "Oedipus cycle" as copious
as your Julian the Apostate poems . . .
You never had much use for "French Modern" wits,
    preferring to get the news from old
    farts and fogies like Anatole France,
        Heredia and Barrès . . .
    Unfortunately, it was the new guys,
    Cocteau and company (how you'd have
despised *ces messieurs!*), who were now dispensing
plays, poems, and theories "on" Oedipus—
    as Gide (one of them) remarked:
    a veritable Oedipemic!
        But to all such contagion
    you were immune, inspired by some wag's
    verbose variations on a theme
of semi-porn bric-a-brac. I wonder . . .
Moreau's wasteland (my turn now: I'm looking
    right at it—a *full-color* postcard
    purveyed by the Metropolitan)

is *riddled*, the saying goes,
with partially eaten corpses of
previous contenders whom the Sphinx,
to put it nakedly, had stumped—did you get
that much? And from the *Revue*'s coverage
could you ever get *the whole picture*?
Could you see that this lynx-girl man-eater
(the human flesh of her one
visible breast as adamantine
as the hero's thigh she perches on)
has clawed away most of his sea-green mantle
to gain a more intimate purchase—if not
an actual embrace then at least
an uninvited, unresisted
eyeball-to-eyeball *stare*? Why?
Has she already put her rather
childish Question? Or has he just made
his famous and really infantile Reply?
What has the Sphinx done (or failed to do) to him?
What will he do to her? Does she seek
her fate in his eyes? In hers he sees
the eager desire he knows

he can slake as he could Jocasta's,
    whose very crown—has he realized?—
this cormorant-wingèd killer also wears.
At first you might have been disappointed by
    that rosy little face (anything
    but the physiognomy of Fate),
        and then could you have made out
    what her tail is clearly pointing to?
    On the bare rock, just beneath her, is
a heap of deep Sphinx do-do, which Moreau
has rendered as a handful of glowing gems:
    the comprehensible outcome of
    the beast's incontinent outrage at
        receiving the right answer.
    And you surmised some dungy event,
    Sphingal *and* sphincteral, had occurred,
for your "Rejected Poem" is quite explicit:
"*Yet he takes no pleasure in his victory.*"
    Whose gaudy journalism told you that?
    According to the *Revue des Deux Mondes*
        Théophile Gautier himself
    had conceded he was "not displeased

by how much Hamlet there seemed to be
in the naked prince." Was that your clue to write:

> *His gaze fills with sadness;*
> *he is blind to the Sphinx*
> *but sees the narrow road*
> *that goes to Thebes and comes*
> *to its end in Colonus.*

Could you have read such things in some *art-critic's*
   gloss on Moreau's grisly *erotik?*
   I don't believe it. Dear Constantine
      (if I may), even by this
   "rejected poem" you had fulfilled
   the Moreau you never saw (never
mind his amiable explicator whom
you happened to read); and when you came to write
   those last lines about your "naked prince":

> *. . . and in his soul there is*
> *a clear foreboding*
> *that there the Sphinx*

will speak to him again
with much more difficult
and far greater riddles
that have no answer

you were looking far enough ahead
           to see what poems you could
reject in favor of those to be
written once you had been purged
of your beginnings: the poems of no myth
or method but of reality, which is
a human imagination of
all that we know to be inhuman.

The Rape of the Daughters of
Leucippus by Castor and Pollux

PETER PAUL RUBENS, 1619

For ages, all of us have had the story wrong,
    and it is probably Pure Folly
to imagine that the time-honored (or time-*shamed*)
    version of this indecorously
illustrious and so often illustrated
    episode can be altered so late
in the day; but Rubens' vision of Truth prevails,
    and misconstruction must give way!
First of all, as far back as Homer we were told
    the name *Dioscuri* (sons of Zeus)
bestowed *late in the day* on Castor & Pollux
    is actually a misnomer:

Castor, whom Leda, in her more conjugal moods,
    liked to say was the Spitting Image

of Tyndareos, the "cuckold king of Sparta"
    (*everyone knew*)—Castor was, of course,
merely a mortal, but Pollux, his so-called "twin,"
    somehow managed to Figure It Out,
i.e., divined he must be more or less divine
    thanks to the Swan-rape (*everyone knew*),
and never let Leda forget What Had Happened,
    hard as the poor deluded dear tried
not to prefer godly traits to human ones, when
    she managed to recognize them.

Once smitten, twice shy, was her odd excuse, adding
    with a little laugh: *Whatever shape*
Fate determines to show . . . I doubt she even knew
    for sure which of her boys was "special,"
and Pollux would never have let her get wind of
    the hard-and-fast bargain he'd driven
with his fast-and-loose Begetter, ensuring that
    on alternate days the *twin heroes*
would share a single immortality, half on
    Olympus and half among the Shades,

though their earthly life would be simultaneous—
a complicity of *marauders*! . . .*

Barely adolescent, the boys manifested
    shameless and fully *shared* hankerings
for violent sexual conquest, beyond doubt
    inherited, honed to mastery
on one another (the mortal prince most often
    took for himself the ravisher's role—
was this, too, a "usual fact"? or merely
    a minimally invasive act:

* Cleaving to Castor, Pollux deplored the after-
        effects of the Swan's exploits; himself
    hatched rather than born (those god-awful gaudy shells,
        not bronzed babybooty but gilded
    —*Leda insisted*—"for sentimental reasons";
        and since displayed through countless aeons
    to travelers like gullible Pausanias
        touring the Historic Sites of Greece),
    while his "false twin," the utterly mortal sibling,
        was compelled, from first breath to last gasp,
    to confront the Usual Facts of human birth
        and consequently of human death.

as far as a god's body might be manhandled?).
    Now, though, at man's estate, both preferred
virgin girls in pairs, taken turn and turn about
    in consummated emulation . . .

How the plains of Sparta echoed to maiden plaints!
    (although not always in demurral),
latterly to those of Leucippus' two daughters,
    Hilaera and Phoebe, long betrothed
to Lynceus and Idas, brothers burning now
    to requite the rape of their brides
on the very morning they were to be married.
    In pitched battle, Castor and the two
expectant bridegrooms would perish
    after the classic violations
in an equally classic revenge, whereupon
    Pollux could deliver his brother,

as Zeus had promised, to an immortality
    every other day. And meanwhile
in another part of the Spartan wilderness,
    Rubens had set (and cleared away)

the scene which led to such funest consequences,
  as well as to the corrigendum
I hereby undertake: *The Rape of the Daughters*
  of Leucippus is not what is here.
Look again, look closer. Those hysterical girls
  are not being, they have already
been raped—they are *being dumped*: Phoebe delivered
  by Castor (in armor and gold chains)

to the ground; Hilaera already there, still braced
  on the knee of naked Pollux, done
with her but still helpful, before leaving to fight
  angry bridegrooms, angrier fathers
altogether elsewhere. Here, the sisters will lie
  in each other's arms a while, shed
a few tears, and then collect their golden rags
  and begin, not talking much, the long
trudge somewhere out of the picture. Ask Leda:
  memory takes some time to compose
itself into a story all of us want to believe,
  although of course it wasn't like that.

Mind Under Matter

Consulting recollection, I am foiled
to find the times I've been honored by love
    chalked up (or down) to purely physical reasons,
as those involved continued to maintain.

This strikes me as wrong-headed, even delusional,
    given (or taking) what the mirror shows.
Why couldn't (and shouldn't) love come to light
    for reasons of . . . well, for *reasons*? Isn't *mind*,

    its faculties, its powers, something worth,
if nothing "purely"—something *more*?
    Dear Robert Browning, what became of . . . love
before what you called kissing could begin?

    Of course my first reaction to what seemed
calumny-by-physique was to rebuke
    the obtuseness of my lovers, if indeed
there were any, actually. And then,

on further reflection (in a different mirror),
  I had to acknowledge that *mind*, insofar as
I know my own, forbears to generate
  high voltage in a lover's interest—

  what could be counted on as competent
erotic apparatus was the lure
  of a strong back and stagnant blue eyes.
Purely physical . . . How sad that is.

Ediya: an interview*

FOR DOROTHEA TANNING

Why don't you set your wicked little machine
on the table. *That's not a question, it's how
queens give commands: Why don't you* . . . No, over *here*
—so that what you mislead me into saying
can be absorbed by your . . . *instrument* without
my having to put Daisy down—how nasty
that sounds. Do set the thing there. *So helpful!*
You see, whatever her Mama does—even
giving an interview—Daisy wants to be
part of the action, don't you, darling?
She likes helping Mama. *So intelligent!*

---

* Interviewer has deleted his questions so that Queen Ediya's remarks, on the
thirtieth anniversary of the Princess Medea's departure from Colchis, might
be more readily comprehended by readers unfamiliar, so long afterward,
with the incidents involved.

Now let's make *sure* we've brought all the things we need.
I *know* that's your job. And I'm *not* suggesting
you're incompetent. But just last week I was
about to respond to your . . . predecessor
when he made me stop and inquired if I had—
"*if I happened to have*," I believe he said—
"an extra tape *around the palace* . . .*" What *is*
a tape? I told him that I never "happened"
to have anything and that queens have nothing
"extra" anywhere. What could he do but leave?

We must never forget that none of us is
infallible—not even the youngest. Now
suppose you start *your* contraption, just to see . . .
If something goes wrong *this* time, we could
always send out for *tapes*, whatever *they* are—
that poor boy seemed to think everyone had some,
didn't he? Now I'll just say a few words. [*Now
I'll just say a few words.*] Wonderful! Let's begin . . .
Daisy, please stop that! She doesn't like machines,
and to be honest with you, neither do I . . .
I side with Daisy—with all dogs, actually,

provided they're small enough to hold on my lap;
you know what I mean, there's a kind of profane
immortality to be achieved by moving
down the scale of such creatures—if that's *down* . . .
(There, she'll be quiet now: no more protesting.)
Of course you're right, it *is* useful: recording
what's been spoken makes for a sort of judgment
on speech, anyone's speech. As we're reminded
each time the police are obliged to warn us:
Whatever you say may be used in evidence
against you. Has that ever happened to you?

Such things are always being said around here;
I can't count how often *I've* been warned . . .
ever since that time they came to question me
—they grilled us all, even poor Aëtes (the King!)—
about Apsyrtus. "*Conflicting evidence,*"
they said: some claimed my boy was part of a plot—
that awful scheme to drug the old dragon and
steal the Golden Fleece . . . truly a glorious thing
—you're much too young to have seen it—but it's just
nonsense to accuse someone *in the family*
of mere thieving—it was ours, *we all loved it!*

You may have noticed (you strike me as being
quite the observant young man) any number
of fine pieces here, some right in this room
—I've added many myself: the caravans
came down to Phasis along the northern route
from Asia with real treasures. Things are such fun!
But that Fleece was the best thing we had. Things do
disappear, though; I live here surrounded by
memories of *everything we used to have.*
Possessions are so much more ephemeral
than people, don't you find? Of course, people *leave* . . .

Medea left, as you must know. (Isn't that why
you're here?) People even die—not Medea,
though: she's at least half immortal—besides,
Medea's too mean to die, she'll always be . . .
admired: for what she *is*. Not like me, oh no!
A woman in my position's admired
for what she's *been*, and for what she's *been through*.
Yet how could I say my daughter's *gone*, the way
things go: always lost—getting lost . . . Old age
has only one lesson to teach about life,
one secret: life is an erotics of absence . . .

So *naturally* Medea was "involved"
in stealing the Fleece—I never did find out
what she did with it. But my boy couldn't have
taken what *belonged* to us (unlike his sister) . . .
And according to some others, Apsyrtus
even led the pursuit of the miscreants,
though still others claim he joined his sister in . . . in . . .
yes, the *Argo*, that's the name—and she killed him
at sea. That's probably the version you heard,
scattered limbs and all the rest . . . We never got
anything like a straight answer, and to this day

that daughter of mine has never once tried to . . .
It's no use asking me the first thing about
Medea. You'd have done better to consult
her late father: Aëtes was a little vague
at the end, and he was always impatient,
but he *knew* so much, if he could just remember
what you asked him. He was a wise man! Even
Circe says so, and it's not every sister
who has praise like that for an older brother!
I gather they were never *close* as children,
but they were both brought up so *peculiarly*!

Of course when your parents are gods . . . I don't know
about those gods—the old families of Colchis
have been here—my father explained this to me
just before my wedding—so much longer than
any of *them*! (So from the start I wanted
to give my children, especially the girls,
a normal home, the kind I was raised in. *That*
didn't come to much.) I don't know—I've never
been able to tell why Aëtes married me:
was it a sort of *social security*?
Why else was he faithful to me . . . if he was?

Like Daisy here, I enjoy my rights, *has she
been Mama's good girl*? But I revel in my
privileges. Which remained in effect till
our first girl was . . . I wonder if Medea
was *born*? Surely I never *had* her. I know
I'm very much like everyone else, but not
really. With Medea, the only peace was
being out of earshot. As she grew (*she did grow*),
my only way of accounting for her was
through the powers of the ordinary, rather
than by the forces of the divine. Of course

I failed. I knew it when she was first learning
to talk: most of us use words to use them up;
our Medea used words so they would remain words.
As a young girl, she was both friendly and cruel.
(She outgrew the friendliness.) And soon I saw
how entirely she belonged to her aunt's side
of the family—I want you to understand
why she turned to Circe and her magic: not
to obscure reality, to *replace* it!
She could stand nothing but intimacy, and
after that—*long after*—formality

or servility; the bad thing of course was
familiarity. As her mere mother,
I could never persuade her that "*I want it*"
is not a moral imperative. One time,
perhaps the last dinner we had together,
the conversation turned, not surprisingly,
to magic means of restoring youth, and I
remember saying I didn't want to be
young again, I wanted to keep growing old . . .
Medea's response was "*if you want to be
a fool, Mother, you've made a fine start.*"

Literally what she said. Her very words.
She could never leave anything alone: each
defect had to be corrected, each detail
attended to, each defeat reversed. And life
without *some* negligence is unbearable.
Of course I hear people say she's a success,
but they mean that everyone's afraid of her.
Which may amount to the same thing, but
I've had the time to remember . . . other things.
You know, eventually one has had enough—
even of oneself. My memories of those

"magic" ceremonies, the ones Circe kept
making her perform for us, are not welcome:
it was all very beautiful and boring: nothing
ever *happened*, figures just melted away,
flickering and fading out like the shadows
from firelight on the wall. In between those awful
incantations came moments when the old witch
(I mean Aunt Circe) would be sure to say in her
most consequential voice: *The time is not yet!*
And then the two of them would burst out laughing,
cackling actually. Those were grim occasions.

And when I warned Medea, who had threatened
to decamp with those Corinthian hoodlums:
Everyone will turn away from you. "I prefer,"
she said, "the backs of their heads." That was Circe,
of course—her style of repartee. I never
saw or heard from her again—Medea, I mean;
Circe reappeared incessantly, spreading
the worst rumors . . . (How many crimes my daughter
had to commit for the news to reach Colchis
—*not* a likely metropolitan target—
within a season of their perpetration!)

. . . In Iolcos, she rejuvenated Jason's
father by boiling him with some herbs
to lure the daughters of Pelias to do
likewise with *theirs* (but giving them the *wrong herbs*:
technically those silly girls were parricides!).
Then there was that unfortunate episode
in Corinth with that poor daughter of Creon's—
of course I don't believe Medea murdered
her own sons?—"reliable sources" saw them
in Athens where she must have left them after
being banished for *trying* to murder Theseus,

or maybe it was Aegeus—I never could
get that part of the story straight. The last
word I had of Medea's whereabouts was
years ago, and from Circe . . . so who knows?
She's now living, *I'm told*, with her son Medus
in some wild country where they've managed to do
away with my late husband's brother Perses
(can you believe it?), and now the place is called
Media! So often the best solution
is to withdraw from the problem, which I did
ages ago. If you've been listening to me

at all, you'll recognize that the compulsion
to repeat—mine *or* Medea's—has replaced
the impulse to remember. It's just as well,
in fact it's much the best thing for all of us.
Usually we don't recognize happiness
until afterward. But that's where I live now:
I live *afterwards*, and my capacity
for staying home (this palace is nine parasangs
from the nearest lemon) and sitting quite still
with Daisy on my lap, has been perfected
and is likely to last the rest of my life.

All I need do is convince Daisy not to scratch
too much. But you know, a certain quantity
of fleas may be good for dogs—at least it keeps
the darlings from brooding about being dogs . . .
Thank you so much for visiting, young man;
I have a notion poor Medea might not be
so eager for us to keep talking about her—
wouldn't she prefer being an Immortal
Secret rather than just the divulgation
of her ancient mother? So why don't we say
the audience—I mean, the interview—is over.

Family Secrets

Climb a rickety stair (better yet, crawl:
steps are missing) up to a garret where
through the one cracked dormer can be observed
all that's left of Ingolstadt . . .
According to his frequent letters home,
my Uncle Walter was billeted there
(not complaining, mind you, just describing)
back in 1944.
I found them in our own Shaker Heights
attic (bearing a close resemblance to
that decrepit Bavarian garret,
except it has more windows),
and in one (letter, not window) I was
amazed to read that Uncle Walter spent
a whole April afternoon *bird-watching*,
all his attention focused on
this one male sparrow—I can't imagine
how my uncle could be so sure (he seemed
absolutely positive) the object

of his attention was male;
don't sparrows of either (or any) sex
look identical? Anyway, he said
he watched this sparrow having intercourse
        twenty times and then dying.
How unfair, Uncle Walter wrote (to my
mother!) *that this is granted to sparrows
and denied to men!* Did he mean it was
        unfair that sparrows could fuck
twenty times, or that men couldn't die
like sparrows after fucking their brains out?
I put the letter back where I found it—
        I didn't feel like asking
anyone (especially my *mother*)
what it was that Uncle Walter meant. Who
was being unfair? To whom? Maybe it had
        something to do with the War.

Exposures

I cannot come to the phone. Please record your message.

Richard? *Richard!* The queerest thing—only
that's *not* what you'd call the *mot juste*, is it?
Okay, the *strangest* thing just happened . . . strange
        to *me* in any case, and
I've got to tell you what I—no, *ask you*
what I should do with it—I mean, maybe
I ought to show the damn thing to the cops?
        I've got to do *something*, but
you're not home, or you're just *not answering*
for some reason, maybe somebody's there,
is that it? But before *I* do anything
        you've got to know what *he* did,
I mean, this *person*. Who else could I mean?
He sat down right across the car from me
—on the Broadway Express, the longest stretch

46

between stations, Times Square to
Seventy-Second, not a soul around—
did I say it was late? Well it was late,
no one was around . . . Oh maybe there was
someone at the other end,
someone fast asleep, but no one watching,
actually looking at the two of us,
not the way *he* was looking at *me*, not
just looking, *staring through me*
and not smiling—frowning! Concentrating
on something *inside me*, that's what I thought
at first, until I realized it was
inside him, and when I looked
away, looked down, *there It was* all right,
free and clear, ready and waiting for me,
or for anyone who had the right *effect*,
I mean, there was no fumbling
with his fly or fidgeting to get It out
of his—could there have been underwear?
Not a clue: It was just *there*, big as life,
nor was he *playing with It*—
what a ridiculous expression! This

was dead serious: no need to touch It
or help It along in any way . . . Richard,
                It didn't need any help—
and I think that's what I resented most.
After all, I wasn't exactly shocked,
I've seen more of those—and at closer range—
                than you've had meals. But I was
dismayed: *he* wasn't looking at me—*It* was!
And I think most women, even the ones
unaccustomed to such exhibitions,
                are put off by the solo
bow, the detached battery, as if
in fact it was merely an attachment—
who can get *attached* to an *attachment?*
                Maybe you men (I mean *gay men*)
manage better because you already
possess such a thing—*prepossession!*
Anyway, all he was up for (to speak
                plainly) was spectator sports,
apparently what his solitary
audience was meant to engage in, and
apparently all that was . . . required.

We must have been at least
past Lincoln Center by then, and . . . nothing!
That was my moment of inspiration.
I had my new cell-phone out, just checking
                which number to call in case
anything bad happened, and then it came
to me, you know? I was as well-prepared
as he was for this *looking* business:
                what you see is what you get,
so I set the damn lens without a glance
and snapped three shots of him—and of *It*!—
before he realized what I had done,
                almost before *I* realized . . .
and then I stood up—*It* was still standing,
free and clear, as I said. I wonder if
a woman *ever* has much to do with
                the fruits of such *posturing*!
It all seemed to be happening to him
—and to *It*—without my involvement
or (saving my uncertain presence) need.
                So what am I, *chopped liver*?
Anyway, there I stood, and as the train

pulled into the station, I just held up my
little cell-phone-camera so he could see
the last picture (mostly *It*)
and smiled and walked out the opening doors
onto the platform and up the stairs and
into the Rose Bar I'm calling you from . . .
Perhaps you'd like me to print
out the three little shots of him (and his
Keepsake) for your own purposes? You might
be pleased with the Sacred Image, you might
even have enjoyed the show . . .
Funny to think that when every briefcase
and baby-carriage is liable to be
inspected for concealed . . . weaponry, such
perilous appendages
can be tacitly worn and openly
deployed. The Way We Live Now: explosives
forbidden unless displayed. As all the signs
on our university doors announce:
YOU MUST SHOW ID TO ENTER.
Who's the wiser—who comes off best? The police,
for another nut case; my showman, for

50

a passing release from his compulsion;
            or me, for turning him in?
Richard, you have to deci . . .

This machine cannot record any further messages.

II. CONCERNING AN INVASION OF PRIVACY

            Richard! You're not there?
    Or not picking up? Well, it's better
            this way: I'll go on talking until
your machine cuts me off, then I'll call you back and talk
            until I'm through. Am I ever through?
    Are you? Who is, really? No one *we* talk to . . .
            Richard, I've had a sort of

            religious experience,
    I think it's called *askesis* (ask anyone
            in Ed Snow's classes: they'll know for sure).
Here's what happened: when I got off the plane at Heathrow
            there was this enormous closet-thing

right in front of the long line of passengers,
           and each of us had to walk

                into it, but no one seemed
       to be coming out the other side—the line
           was single-file, and I was too near
the end to be certain, but I couldn't help thinking
              of the showers at Auschwitz—I knew
this was England and everything, but the line
            and the rain and that great big

              locker we had to go into
one by one really spooked me . . . But then this man
          behind me must have heard the start of
one of my asthma attacks and was kind enough to
           explain what was going on: it seems
BOAC has recently been experimenting
              with a new Security

              System—some folks prefer it
      to being *patted down*, the old way; he said
          that ominous closet-contraption

doesn't release Zyklon-B but actually beams
low-level X-rays through people's clothes!
It's called a Backscatter Body Scanner, and
it produces explicit

images of our bodies—
not revealing bones or gold fillings in teeth,
but every inch of our nakedness
and whatever's fastened on that we try to sneak in:
ceramic knives, that's one example,
and plastic explosives *à fleur de la peau* . . .
I've never worn a gun

or even an iron bra
like Madonna, but I'm sure I'd rather be
patted down than have all my . . .

No further messages can be recorded.

Richard,
I *have* been undressed (not strip-searched, of course) and under
the right circumstances, that can be

entertaining, but I will not be *exposed*.
So I left the line and made

one of my *scenes*, after which
I was taken to a *filthy* dressing-room
where I managed to prove I was
not a terrorist. The "matron" who examined me
said other "ladies" had tried
to protest, but that I was the first to get
my way: does that sound like me?

I was then coolly informed
that the British lead the world in creating
a Surveillance Society—and
when I asked about radiation risks (tactfully
skirting my more *intimate* concerns),
I was told "there is no truly safe
level of radiation."

Which *must* alter the balance
between Security and the Privacy

Issue in favor of the latter,
wouldn't you think? As you know, I'll be here in London
for a few days, and I don't suppose
they'll employ the Backscatter Body Scanner
on *departing* passengers . . .

With luck I can rely on
the U.S. to be lax on Security
and get home without violating
the secret Victoria and I share, keeping which
is one religion any woman
practices. And isn't recognizing
sacrilege (by which I mean

my feeling of outrage caused
by that Backscatter Body Scanner)
somehow recovering the meaning
of the Sacred? Richard, didn't I tell you it was
a religious experience? Would you please
save this message for me: I'd like to read it
over and avoid making

a fool of myself next time
I drop *askesis* or *sacrilege*
around Ed Snow and Co. We'll
talk once I'm back in one (unrecognizable) piece . . .
Meanwhile I'm sending you all my love
from foreign parts, apparently so
different from the other kind.

Bad Tölz, Bavaria, 1909

The demonic should always be addressed poetically; to confront
it by critical essays strikes me as indiscreet. THOMAS MANN,
from an introduction to Dostoievsky's short novels

"The one impression
I received, not just from moment to moment
and from place to place (weren't there too many
rooms on each floor?), but even after leaving
my distinguished host
                              —especially then—
was of someone uncommonly well-groomed
whose elegance was not so much personal
as an attribute of class he had long since
assimilated.
                    Easy to forget
the great man is my own age, even a year
younger. How could Thomas Mann *not* be
my senior? Everything about him seemed so
settled: for instance,

how resolutely
(not permitting a single muscle to yield
to a less decisive expression), perhaps
even *how reverently* he had explained
'this is where I work,'
closing behind us
the oak door to what was no doubt his study
where we would spend a proper hour together
once he had shown me over the entire house,
even the Boys' Room:
'Of course they don't live
at home now, but we haven't found a better
name for it . . .' No one else seemed to be 'at home'
either, especially my host, who expressed
amazement at each
deep oriental,
each dark oil-painting. His house, like Mann himself,
seemed to have achieved perfection *already*,
and no further developments were to be
anticipated.
The only thing, though . . ."

—And here von Hofmannsthal broke off, looking down
at his fingernails (his constant gesture of
embarrassment ever since he had given
in his early teens
                those public readings
of his all-too-private necromantic poems)—

". . . was that in a little side-room Doktor Mann
had overlooked, there happened to be lying
on the clean matting,
              right there, a dead cat."

School Days

Dear Mrs. Masters, Hi! all over again
from the Fifth-Grade Class of Park School. We're home now
                                    from New York City,
where we found out how to balance the neck with
the tail of our model Diplodocus, from
                    the head curator
of the Natural History Museum
(we can do it with a swivel, just the way
                              they do—he showed us!)
and now we don't have to worry any more
about Arthur Englander making our
                    dinosaur collapse
whenever he comes near it. You remember
about David Stashower *biting* Arthur so
                              he would keep away,
and you called a Middle-School Assembly to tell
everyone that biting's no good? Only now

Arthur's done something
worse than ever, and our whole Class has voted
to report What Happened. You see, there was
                    this big male peacock
(they look great this time of year—the way their necks
glisten is even better than when they spread
          those tail-feather "eyes":
last week we saw a whole flock of these birds
strutting and posing in the Central Park Zoo) . . .
                    Anyway, this bird
managed to get inside our School parking lot
—just wandered in through the open gate, I guess—
          and the attendant
was feeding him bread (out of his own lunchbox)
which was easy to do because the peacock
                    had conveniently
perched on the hood of a purple Pierce-Arrow
(it was actually standing right *on* that
          chromium Archer).
Mrs. Masters, did you know that someone here
in Sandusky *raises* peacocks? His name is
                    Felice Finnegan,

and he's been doing it for years—he sells them
to parks and zoos and sometimes gives them to friends:
a woman who lives
near Park School has six or seven of his birds
but none of them ever managed to escape
until this one did,
although he seemed quite tame and willing to stay
on that car-hood, eating bread out of the hand
of anyone who would
feed him. After What Happened, someone called
that Felice Finnegan, who came right over
to the parking lot:
he told us this bird was ten years old (which is
the same age as us) but didn't know better.
Know better than what?
Mr. Sanchez (that's the parking attendant)
said he—the peacock, not Mr. Sanchez—would
have gone on eating
bread all day long, but then Arthur Englander
(of course Mr. Sanchez didn't know his name:
Duncan Chu told him)
came out of nowhere as if he already

heard the peacock was there on the Pierce-Arrow
                        and ran right over
and grabbed him by that beautiful neck, dragged him
down to the gravel and started kicking and
                stomping the poor bird
which once Arthur got a hold of him began
screaming and then Mr. Sanchez was screaming, and
                        even Arthur was
screaming, I guess. Pretty soon the peacock
was so badly beaten most of his tail feathers
                had fallen out, but
he wasn't dead yet, just lying on the ground
thumping his wings and trying to get away from
                        Arthur Englander.
That was when Felice Finnegan came, and *he*
started screaming too, but screaming at Arthur:
                "What are you doing?
Are you nuts?" and Arthur screamed back: "Can't you see?
let me finish, this has to be done right, I'm
                killing a vampire!"
And right then Felice Finnegan did something
which made the peacock stop screaming and struggling—

I think it died then,
but by the time Felice Finnegan had called
the police—they came right away, they're always
                    somewhere around school—
Arthur was Nowhere To Be Found. However
Duncan Chu was able to give them Arthur's
                    address—he lives with
some relative who looks after him, sort of.
(Duncan Chu isn't a snitch, he knows all our
                    names and addresses
the way he knows Chinese and math—it's the way
his mind works: lists and tables are just in there.)
                    Mrs. Masters, our
whole Fifth-Grade Class unanimously voted
to report What Happened because we all think
                    Arthur Englander
should be punished, maybe expelled from Park School—
we all know for a fact he doesn't even
                    believe in vampires,
no one in our Class does—not enough to kill
a tame ten-year-old peacock for being one.
                    Arthur Englander
doesn't believe in anything, he just likes

destroying things—if our Diplodocus were
       alive, he'd kill it!
Our whole class believes that dinosaurs—all
dinosaurs, not just our own Diplodocus—
                are alive somewhere
on earth, and both Lucy Wensley and Nancy
Akers have heard Arthur say he wants to kill
       some of the big ones
wherever they are: he was warming up on
Felice Finnegan's bird. We are asking you
            to expel Arthur
and buy the peacock lady *another* bird
(not one that's already ten years old—a chick
       would be fine with us:
we could feed it bread and watch it grow). No one
in our Class, I told you, believes a peacock
           could be a vampire,
or even really believes in vampires. So
please, Mrs. Masters, expel Arthur from school
       or at least put him
in some other Class. This request has been signed
unanimously by the entire Fifth Grade,
          we hope to hear from you . . .

Dear Mrs. Masters, as you probably know,
almost half our Fifth-Grade Class is Jewish—not
    a majority
but *lots*, without even counting our teacher
Miss Husband, who's getting married (next June) to
    a *gentile husband*!
—that has to change more than her name, doesn't it?
Well, your office records must show who's really
    Jewish and who's not,
and for some of us who just *happen to be*
Jewish, those records might be the only sure
    indication of
our race or faith or whatever makes us Jews,
and therefore different from the other kids
    (no one really knows).
But this week our Rabbi told us this weird thing:
he says there are Jews—mostly in Hasidic
    congregations and
they're mostly in Brooklyn—who perform (between
Rosh Hashana and Yom Kippur) this ritual

called *pekkarot*—no,
that's backward, the Hebrew word is *kapparot*—
during which Believers swing a live chicken
        high over their heads:
this whirling is meant to transfer the Hasid's
sins to the chicken, which is then sacrificed.
        Rabbi Abraham
said about 50,000 chickens are used
in these ceremonies all over Brooklyn—
        that's a lot of birds
to get slaughtered (after being whirled), and most
wind up in someone's pot. Not everyone whirls
        chickens, there are some
Orthodox Believers who whirl money instead—
Maimonides himself once called *kapparot*
        a pagan practice
that should be abandoned, but our Rabbi says
it's going strong in Brooklyn and can't be stopped.
        Now Mrs. Masters,
we've learned—trust Duncan Chu to find out, of course—
that Arthur Englander's late parents
        were Hasidic Jews

(Arthur was the boy who killed that peacock, but
you wouldn't punish him, even though we voted
          unanimously
to expel him from the Fifth Grade), and when we
went to see his Aunt, she showed us a photo
          of Arthur, age six,
wearing gloves and whirling a big white rooster
for *kapparot* . . . No one knew where he had gone
          after What Happened,
but you said he we should help him "find himself"
if he came back to Park School, and of course
          the police found him
right away. Mrs. Masters, we think Arthur
believed he had to slaughter that poor peacock
          for his *kapparot*—
he got it all mixed up with vampire movies
and that's what he meant when he screamed
          he had to do it
right. Christine Rath says that's how religions work.
Even when we've forgotten what they mean
          we do what we think
are the same things people have always done.

But we forget. Or we change. And Christine's
                    not even even Jewish!
And then Duncan Chu said that religions die
once they're proved to be true. And that Science is
                    the tombstone of dead
religions. And Duncan's not Jewish either.
But David Stashower is, so he had to
                    tell what his father
thinks: that Scientists now say the same thing
as Rabbis, but without capital letters.
            Arthur Englander
paid no attention to what anyone had said,
but now most of us want him back in Fifth Grade
                    with all the others.

III. A FIFTH-GRADE PROTEST

Dear Mrs. Masters, When the School Year began
you said we could—no, you said we *should* tell you
            if something happened
in class that made us feel bad. Well, now it has,

two times, so we're telling. You know Mr. Lee,
                    the Science teacher?
—he's told us to call him Dinny, we don't know
his real first name, but we *like* calling him that:
                    no other teacher
lets us use a nickname the same way we do
with each other—you know, like Micky and Nan
                    and all the others—
Dinny likes inviting to class Special Guests
from all over the State and even outside
            who can show us things,
even passing them around from hand to hand—
things we may never have seen, like animals
                    from the jungle, or
baby animals that can't be taken away
from their mothers for very long . . . Just last month
            a Mr. Schwartz came,
he's a pig-farmer and he brought a piglet—
only for an hour, he said it had to go
                    back to its litter
soon, but each of us could hold it a minute.
It was an albino, which means it was all

white, except the eyes:
they were pink under long white eyelashes.
It all started when the piglet squealed because
                    Duncan Chu held it
too tight, and left him a nice big lapful of
little pink pellets, in revenge. By that time
          our whole Fifth-Grade class
was getting just a little worried about
the piglet's being kept too long from the sow
                        (that's the mother pig),
so Mr. Schwartz gave it some milk and put it
back in its black (pigskin) bag and took it home.
          That was the first time
we got upset—the whole class: you see, next day
Dinny told us that as soon as Mr. Schwartz
                    put our piglet back
in the pen, the mother pig *ate* it right there
while she was nursing the rest of her litter!
          How could she do that?
Dinny tried to explain to us that the sow
did not realize the piglet was gone, but
                    had found something wrong

with it once it was back, because everyone
had held it, and that's when Jane McCullough and
　　　　Nancy Akers and
Jeanne Sturgess started crying, and Duncan Chu
said everyone should have been wearing gloves—
　　　　　　　　and from that point on
we all got really upset. Mrs. Masters,
we don't want sows eating their piglets just
　　　　because they visited
the Fifth-Grade class of Park School. And the next thing
that happened was even worse. Much worse!
　　　　Dinny invited
this man he knew, Mr. Van Allmen, to bring
his 14-foot reticulated python
　　　　　　　　to our Science Class
so we could discover for ourselves that snakes
were not slimy at all, but clean and friendly;
　　　　he told us they made
very good pets actually, always being
"tractable" (meaning *manageable*) when they've
　　　　had enough to eat.
He requested volunteers to hold "Rajah"

(the perfect name for an Indian python,
            even though stupid
Arthur Englander kept calling him Roger),
but out of the whole class only the Klein twins
                  (and Dinny, of course)
would let him drape Rajah around their shoulders
the way Mr. Van Allmen did, once he had
        pulled the python out
of his cage. It was a good (though scary) class—
we learned a lot about what pythons eat,
                  how they hatch from eggs
and live many years longer than human beings
unless hunted and killed for their high-priced skins.
        That class was last week,
but today Dinny told us Rajah's owner
was found crushed to death in a backyard shed
                  near Lanesville, about
fifteen miles west of Sandusky. A medical
examiner said "death was consistent with
        asphyxiation
caused by compression of the neck and chest."
Apparently Ohio law does not restrict

ownership of snakes,
so Rajah was returned to Mr. Van Allmen's
family. How could they take him, after that?
Mrs. Masters, how
could *we* take any more visitors like that?
There must be some other way Dinny could teach
us about Nature
without our having to learn that mother pigs
eat their babies, and that pythons have to kill
their owners, even
when given enough to eat. As members of
the Fifth-Grade Class of Park School, we protest
against such instruction;
we're asking to learn less about death and more
about life—isn't that what *biology*
is supposed to mean?
Please arrange for Dinny Lee not to invite
visitors like that any more. I don't think
the class can take it.

Dear Mrs. Masters,
The Fifth-Grade Class of Park School herewith submits
our Research Project for the year 2000.
                              In choosing our theme
              we have attempted
to follow guidelines Miss Husband provided,
noting first of all our Project's special date,
                        which appears to be
              widely regarded
as a sort of turning point in History,
and secondly the Official School Mandate
                        that every Project
              have some bearing on
Life As It Is Actually Lived on Earth.
This seems to include whatever our Class
                        (or any other)
              could hypothesize.
We did notice, though, that all the previous
Fifth-Grade-Class Research Projects we consulted
                        dealt exclusively

with Past Achievements,
so therefore, on account of this year being
a Millennium, *our* Fifth-Grade Class voted
unanimously
to concentrate on
what the Future might have in store for us—how
the Millennium's prospects and promises
may relate to us.
What inspired us most,
as you are about to learn, was a field trip
our Class made recently to the Reptile House
of the Cleveland Zoo.
But before we tell
what we learned there about *Life ... Lived on Earth*,
you should know (you probably do already—
it's a Required Course)
that our Fifth-Grade Class
has also taken this year what the Office
calls the *Hygiene Concentration* (most of us
prefer calling it
something different),
where we learned about Sexual Intercourse

between Men & Women. Some Class members claim
they knew already,
but according to
Miss Husband, most people know *different things*
about S.I., and what Promotes Fulfillment
in Sexual Life
(her actual words)
is that everybody should know the *same things*.
Well, for us this has been what Miss Husband calls
a challenging term,
because the whole Class
finds it hard to believe that grownup people
voluntarily subject themselves to such
stupid behavior
(which Miss Husband says
they must, in order to produce children) and
expect to gain some form of pleasure by
taking part in it.
Some girls in our Class—
Lois Hexter and Lucy Wensley, for instance,
claim the film we were shown and the "clinical"
vocabulary

Miss Husband employed
to describe what invariably goes on
during S.I. made the whole thing seem
                    disagreeable,
          to say the least, and
sometimes really disgusting. All three Davids:
Stashower, McConnahey and Halperin,
                    refuse to believe
          that their parents did
(even *once*) some of the things we saw and heard
just to have us; they claim they'd have heard
                    their parents *complain*.
          Dear Mrs. Masters,
perhaps now you can understand how, after
the disturbing revelations of Hygiene,
                    our Class responded
          to the Vision of
a Future Free from the horrors of S.I.—
we first discovered this on our field trip to
                    the big Reptile House
          of the Cleveland Zoo
just before Christmas vacation. They have these

Komodo Dragons there—the biggest lizards
                              on earth, ten feet long,
                dinosaurs really,
solitary monsters which come together
only for mating which the keepers say is
                              so horrifying
                to watch they now keep
each Dragon in a separate cage. Here's what
happens, according to eyewitness accounts:
                              first the male vomits
                to prepare himself,
then he flicks his tongue at the female to judge
her "receptivity"; usually she resists
                              with her claws and teeth—
                he has to pin her
to the ground during S.I. (with lizards
it's called *coitus*) to avoid being hurt.
                              The keepers told us
                that after S.I.
it takes a Dragon Mom seven months to hatch
a clutch of some 20 eggs, and after that
                              it takes five years for

young Dragons to reach
maturity—*maturity* means eating
baby Dragons (10% percent of their diet)
which have to become
fast tree-climbers to
"avoid predation" (a zoo expression for
not getting themselves devoured by Dragon Dad).
We can all see why
zoos keep males apart
from females, and therefore why it must have been
quite a surprise for everyone involved,
two years ago, when
this one female laid
a clutch of fertile eggs that actually hatched
by a process called *parthenogenesis*—
it means they don't *need*
S.I. with the males.
(This also happens, one keeper informed us,
with certain fish.) Well, what we'd like to know is:
could Science obtain
similar results
in *humans*? If female Dragons can avoid

the discomforts and damages of S.I.
by sheer willpower
(that's what it *looks like*),
can't something of the kind be achieved *for us*?
Mrs. Masters, this is what our Class Project
would like to propose
as its conclusion
(with the assistance of Medical Science):
a vision of Human Life without S.I.—
a New and Improved
Version we conceived
after contemplating the probable course
of our grown-up lives in the years to come. These
Komodo Dragons
(as we can tell from
the hatchlings' evolved stratagem of climbing
trees to escape their own parents' appetites)
are a high enough
form of life—higher
than "certain fish"—to provide Modern Science
a model for an ameliorated
Human Existence.

Dear Mrs. Masters,
with the exception of Anne Wiebe,
who is Catholic and therefore insists, quite
erroneously,
we have now learned,
that there can be only a Single Incidence
of parthenogenesis in *life as*
it is lived on Earth),
the whole Fifth-Grade Class
of Park School is proud to present this Project
for the Future well-being of Human Life.
Perhaps one of us
in this very Class
will be able to relieve humanity
of the burden of sexual intercourse.
We strongly hope so.
(signed)
Yours Faithfully,

Judy Abrams, Nancy Akers, Duncan Chu
Arthur Englander, David Halperin, Jane

McCullough, Lois
Hexter, Lucy Wensley,
David McConnehey, David Stashower,
Jeanne Sturges, Kenneth & Jonathan Klein
Michael Hopkinson

Notes of an Industrious Apprentice, or
What the Master Knew

from the London diary of Hugh Walpole, April 1911

FOR ROBERT GOTTLIEB, IN AT THE

BEGINNING AND AT THE CULMINATION

OF THESE MUTUAL CONCERNS

THURSDAY EVENING

My first impression, the poor aftermath
of a bewildering minute, was that our
hostess—I had never been her guest
before this afternoon—was overdressed
for the occasion; by the time I left
I realized it was the rest of us
who had failed to dress appropriately . . .

"I've called you here in order to confess
our utter failure—how unfortunate
yet unavoidable that I must be obliged
to bring this sorry news to valued friends
who have so long and loyally sustained
my little scheme to secure for Mr. James
the proper honor of a Nobel Prize" . . .

These words were spoken not an hour ago
so all the "valued friends" might realize
how disappointed Mrs. Wharton was
by *our* "utter failure" to consummate *her*
"little scheme," as she was pleased to call
the tangled web of testimonials
ranging from Sir Edmund Gosse (who else

so likely to switch on the Northern Lights?)
to *"dull Dean Howells, the one safe*
American luminary—most of us"
(Mrs. Wharton summed up her countrymen)
"so unrestrained, so dubious, so odd,"
and from her quite nonplussed Ambassador
in Stockholm to Our Man in Downing Street

(perhaps not *her* man at all, considering
the tact needful to pocket a Prix Nobel:
if most MPs tell their wives Secrets of State,
Asquith tells them to other people's wives).
Yet even here Mrs. Wharton had devised
an antidote to any subterfuge
that might be taken as *louche* or untoward:

"Such a cunning letter Paul Bourget
wrote for us to the Committee—it gave
those people (who knows who they are?
Swedes, of course, but how do such Swedes read?)
precisely the right pan-European touch
to win the only homage worthy of
the only Master, our own Henry James!"

Yet now she stood before us, gravely gowned,
announcing to our mutual dismay
that all these infallible tools had *"utterly failed,"*
and all *we* could do, apparently, was drink
a little more of her very good champagne
as she described in tortuous detail
the shameful rationale of *"our defeat."*

The Wharton spies had reported that it was
"problems with English" (the English of Henry James)
which led the Swedes "*to groom a candidate*
whose artless French enjoys a flashy vogue"
—our hostess warming to her poignant theme—
"*in theaters from Paris to Petersburg*
and all points west; a so-called 'Symboliste'

whose Oiseau bleu, *sufficiently inane*
for a Christmas panto, opens this very week
in the West End—no more! The wretched choice
is made and must not be divulged until
the Academy is ready to announce
its honors in other fields. My sorry news
is that Henry James has been passed over

for the 1911 Nobel Prize in Literature
in favor of a writer known (in Belgium) as
the Belgian Shakespeare, Maurice Maeterlinck."
Tableau!—conceive our hostess, half in tears
and half in high contempt, suggestive of
Satan amid his downcast followers,
many wondering who the bugger was.

I knew, of course—why didn't she?—about
the Master's fond allusion to Maeterlinck
(herewith chapter and verse from *Wings of the Dove*):
"*Such the twilight that gathers about them now
like some dim scene in a Maeterlinck play.
We have the image, in the delicate dusk,
of personages coalesced yet so opposed*"

—it's the moment Millie sees through Kate at last—
"*the angular pale Princess, ostrich-plumed,
black-robed and hung about with amulets,
quite still against the slowly circling Lady
of her Court who must exchange with her,
across black water streaked with evening gleams,
fitful questions and answers.*" What a gaffe—

an insult, really—to take no notice of
the Master's wonderful citation. How
could a serious devotee have missed
oh, not the point (she never misses points,
angles, anything acute), but a *mirage*
of life with all the blur of Being on it . . .
Mr. James had seen it distinctly enough

to take the Maeterlinck shadows for his own,
a vision that he sanctioned, savored, *shared*!
I wonder . . . Would the Master really care
all that much about missing a Nobel Prize
if he "happened" to learn he *had* just missed it?
In Henry James, people are always missing things,
and it seems that what it is they miss *they have*!

Was Mrs. Wharton's will that the world accede
to her Great Friend's greatness so imperative
she must "secure" that Prize for him as if
it were the world? Consider those dim
recipients among its first ten years:
Sully-Prudhomme, Lagerlöf, Mistral and Kipling—
Kipling! The Master to follow that . . . machine!

I think it's Mrs. Wharton who cares so much;
that's why she insists the Master not *find out* . . .
Such machinations—such futility!
Our helpless little coven dribbled away,
and in our ears a last haggish drawl
of discontent, the concluding caveat
to all of us: "*Not a Word to Anyone.*"

And of course *his* words (by afternoon post)
were at my door, the kind of coincidence
worthier of Ouida than of Henry James:
the Master's wildly alliterative appeal
for "help" (my help!) at the first performance of
Maeterlinck's *Bluebird* next Saturday week,
on which heroic occasion "we" are to host

the dramatist *and* his diva, Georgette Leblanc,
who is his mistress too: the Master alludes
to the poor lady as "*so much more, as well*
as matrimonially less, than any mere
(and imaginary) Mme. Maeterlinck"—
the four of us to have the Manager's Box
at Saturday's Haymarket matinee. I guess

Mrs. Wharton had got wind—from Mr. James
himself?—about such giddy outings. *Item*:
the dinner in Paris with Minnie and Paul Bourget
which must have begot this new *entente cordiale* . . .
Why else did she keep *at* me so about
not telling: "*Dearest Hugh, you know how much*
he admires your ... work, how fond of you he is,

so you will *be particularly careful not*
to let this piece of awful news slip out—
we must protect the dear man while we can,
even at those moments when it seems
only fair that someone we're so fond of
should know whatever we ourselves may know . . .
Promise me I can count on you . . . " As if

I was uniquely likely to release
her wretched cat from its now-empty bag
or was somehow less safe with a secret than her friends
who are as reliable as a flock of parrots—
I've actually heard Walter Berry claim
"*Without gossip, humanity would become*
not animals but vegetables!" Mr. James

has never coaxed a confidence from me,
for all our "closeness," and our intercourse
has always been as free and easy as if
it were between equals, which both of us
know perfectly well it is not! The friendship is
something of a mystery, I suppose, and
had better remain one, although

I can't help thinking what the Master likes
is to be *seen about* with me, as if
in fact he's showing me off, or putting us both
on stage . . . Just now and then. Of course it's not
as if I were "the heir" or the "coming thing":
I'm quite convinced he has no use at all
for what I've written so far, or even anything

I'll ever write. Nevertheless, I *do* like being
with him, listening to him, knowing that he
listens to me—would he ask so many questions
if he weren't really listening? Even so,
the price (I mean the *cost* to vanity)
is prohibitive at times. *Item*:
"*Only last night, dearest Hugh, I read*

your Maradick at Forty, *which quite failed*
to alter me from the grim and battered old
critical *critic I remain—it seems*
as irreflectively juvenile as your first,
a monument to the abuse of dialogue
and to the absence of all other phases
of presentation than the dialogic—

and yet it's all so lovable—*though not*
so written. *It's not written, darling Hugh,*
at all! *You've never got expression tight*
& in close quarters with your subject, which
remains loose and far. But can you forgive
all this from your fondest, truest old HJ?"
Of course I can. I must. I also must,

the Master stipulates, "be on my best
French behavior." *My* French! So stiff,
what other kind but the best could I be on
with a foreigner who has—or will have soon—
gained (unguessed by an applauding world)
the eleventh Nobel Prize for literature,
escorted by his vanquished rival who

may or may not (but "must not") know who knows
if anyone *else* knows whatever *he* may know . . .
How Jamesian an occasion it will make,
so many mysteries never to be solved
but measured merely—merely!—*as* mysteries:
miasmal Maeterlinck and his *mâitresse*,
myself and the Master, apparently immersed

in *L'Oiseau bleu*, participating in
a moment seemingly shared without a shred
of past alloy or future likelihood
to lead up to, or lure away from, what
the Master likes to call The Real Right Thing,
a phrase by which he almost always means
an overwhelming sense of All Gone Wrong . . .

SATURDAY AFTERNOON

The boxkeeper—just my age, as I would learn,
and fine-featured but for a comical nose—
explained in a superfluous whisper (the play
was not *about* to begin) what would be
obvious once he opened the box: our guests
were *here*, though they had somehow arrived
without tickets (surely left for them *somewhere!*)

and insufficient English to show cause
for being there. "Madam kept 'issin'

Say sa pyess ah louie, sa prowpre pyess!
That's French, innit? I thought the words
sounded so much like 'Open Sesame'
I let 'em in the box. I din't do
nothin' wrong, did I? . . . " Though syntax is

no shallow part of what makes us human,
the fellow's double negative could not
(wholly) dim the lure of "Open Sesame" . . .
Why wait until the interval? I gave
Ali Baba (my intentions altogether
innocent) a sovereign for his pains,
whereupon (an adverb for Romance—

in Drama *the hero acts*, in mere Romance
things happen to the hero, in this case me),
"whereupon" he gently squeezed my hand,
leaving there a grimy pellet which,
furtively unfurled, read *"What's Up when we
Come Down?"* This must be Romance for real!
Lust will find a way: after Act V

(I had been warned) the Master would escort
his notables to Simpson's for a chop,
(or perhaps two: nothing miasmal about Monsieur,
who looked to me as fleshy and vermeil
as a Flemish rose). So that after Madame
had artlessly asked her host if "*lui aussi
écrivait des pièces?*" and the Master, his

reply once composed, had murmured to me
how much he was "vulgarly enjoying Georgette";
and when, after Monsieur had confided
(apparently to Madame) that *Meestair Jame*
spoke the purest French to be heard *en ce pays*
"*même plus pur que le tien, ma chérie*",
their chop was cooked, and "darling Hugh"

no longer needed in order to cement
the gaiety of nations: I could be
released as the dispensable stripling
I become once quantities are known.
Then, on some subsequent occasion when
we are "alone together" once again,
the Master will fill in the blanks for me

—there are always blanks in intercourse
with anyone but himself, and he does love
filling them in. Who else could do it as well?
Perhaps it is the failure of the world itself
to be "complete" in Henry James's sense
that is the source and secret of his art,
indeed of what's become his whole pursuit:

that marvelous compensation for the mere
gaps and fissures of human intercourse,
all the dropped stitches of our life. *Item*:
"*A curious thing, dear Hugh, once you had left*
for the exercise of devices all your own,
how at our diner en ville *the poet seemed*
to grow, a magical metamorphosis!

extraordinarily big and red and rough
as to surface—somehow he underwent
a curious physical coarsening, though still
most genial and pleasant: I had the sense
of our talking over a palisade, or through
a window, as it were, so that he might
defenestrate at any given moment;

yet for all his meaty modifications, I
found 'Maurice' accommodating enough
—we had reached that pitch of camaraderie
in ink and Vouvray at which the stagey pair
insisted I must answer to 'le Sieur Henri'
and, being accommodating myself, I did—
I found, I say, both Maeterlinck and his

semi-conjugal companion quite sympa,
as you would say in your curtailing way,
though of course I resisted probing either one
to the probably disgraceful depths below . . ."
But that was all the Master's *fun*, a theme
for unrivaled variations in the key
of outrage and urbanity, devised

post mortem (recollected in malignity,
so to speak) for my amusement and,
of course, his own. What *I* was now compelled
to offer at the Haymarket, was not
a show of patience, merely, but a sort
of affirmation kindred to applause
for a ritual exercise of persiflage

(predictable in spirit if not in form)
of literary veterans inured
to coping with the carefully rehearsed
illustrations of each other's oddity—
"no two alike," as father used to say.
It was the prospect of the Master's mirth—
not what he laughed at presently but what

his smile foretold: he smiles, these days, for no
incentive other than the promise or
the prospect of expression; when the Word
occurs within him, surfaces, incites
the bliss of some oncoming utterance—
I've learned to read such messages into
or out of the Master's surreptitious smile,

and for that very reason must have laughed
quite audibly, anticipating larks
to come, and of course from Maeterlinck received,
—precisely when the Chorus of the Unborn
[*offstage*] was giggling its head or heads off
(those Babies were *loud*)—this stern rebuke:
"*Le seul vrai rire, c'est le rire enfantin*,"

at which pronouncement (issued with all
the visionary candor of a childless man),
Mme. Leblanc, whose union with Monsieur
must be profound indeed, threw back her head,
exposing an acre of nacreous neck,
and loosed the loudest peal of derisive mirth
ever heard in the Haymarket, on stage or off.

But all this was a minor commotion, not
my real dilemma: tell the horrid news
or cherish a sworn-to silence, just the sort
of problem more readily solved by Henry James
(the Master indeed of covenants betrayed
and guilty consciences susceptible
to ceaseless scruple) than by tyro Hugh

wriggling on his rickety gilt chair
in a garish playhouse lockup which encaged
feral grown-ups only French could tame.
Meanwhile *The Bluebird's* grim *enfantillage*
twittered past us all, and here was I
anything but primed to keep My Secret
(how could I be, not yet *post the Prix?*)

"encaged" myself by what I knew and what
I couldn't guess—certainly not from postures
of the impervious Master listening hard
or of the impassive Maeterlinck listening soft:
did either one of *them* "know" anything?
Whatever promises I'd made to Our
Lady of Manipulations, could I now,

after last week's disclosures, keep *to myself*
just who had "gained the gold" (our scoffing phrase
for honors dealt to *someone else* at school—
quite proper for the Dynamiter's Prize):
the "*Symboliste*" now seated cheek by jowl
(how else, with those dewlaps?) beside his more
—oh much more!—meritorious host, and from

all evidence—or actually from none at all—
as unaware of even the likelihood
of Swedish tribute as was the Master himself
of being "passed over" (Mrs. Wharton's term) . . .
That same Master who in one of those spells
of inestimable silence which drowned out
Maurice's dialogue, leaning past Georgette,

so dapper in her turban and as blessedly
deaf to English as Vermeer's girl in hers,
whispered to me (doesn't Edith Wharton herself
describe them as *proscenium whispers?* How many
she must have endured as he helped her
work herself free—a frightfully costly move—
of her Difficult Marriage to Poor Dear Teddy)

. . . whispered how fondly he hoped I would enjoy
"the rest of the evening, whatever shreds and shards
you've shored up for yourself." Uncanny man!
Are there no secrets from his imagination?
(It must have limits, even rules, but we
can only imagine what they are.) How much
had he divined from our . . . signals exchanged

in the most hugger-mugger of semaphors
about my later *rendez-vous* with Bert
(his name of course is Albert, but perhaps
he prefers not being reminded, every time,
of a Prince Consort's role). Yet how discreet
I thought I'd been! As if I needed proof
that nothing is ever lost on Henry James

who repeatedly sees the exception before
he knows the rule. I'm not at all clear
where the line is which (or so we're told)
sharply divides white magic from black.
Except when he speaks to me in sentences
like scissors (almost always scissors about
my writing) I swim in the melted butter of

his attention, though after so much churning
the mere silent presence of butter itself
may seem an anticlimax. *Item*: When,
as now, he refers to choices we may not share,
for almost nothing about them can be exchanged:
bed and board with a vengeance, i.e.,
bored in bed by life with boys like Bert!

SATURDAY NIGHT, VERY LATE

Inquisitive Bert has only just left, and apart
from easy answers: "*My elderly friend
is an American writer ... No, by the Flemish
gentleman ... Not his wife, but she performs*

in every play he writes ... Both of them are
famous all over Europe and will soon be
more so . . ." I don't suppose I gave him much

satisfaction—certainly not half so much
as he gave me; but all the same, I was
good for a fiver, which may have done the trick.
I must have begged instead of answering
the other questions—posers, some of them.
He wanted to know, for instance, why I laughed,
or tried so hard not to (what sharp eyes he has!)

when Georgette, as I explained, had actually
asked the Master if "he too" wrote plays.
The humor of that I couldn't explain to Bert,
not in English he would understand,
and the Master's reply in Magisterial French
(pure as it was) gave even Georgette no clue
to the long cortège of Magisterial flops.

Pity poor Bert, witnessing such a scene
through a hole in the door (or as the Master says,

"an aperture in the arras," permitting himself
an echo of *Hamlet*, Act III, Scene iv);
it's hard on a boy like that just to *see*
what's going forward and getting nothing back . . .
A writer like the Master (but when was there

ever such a writer?) doesn't *need* to see
to *realize* it all. Oh he must have seen
things once, even if only once, *done* things
for himself, once upon a time . . . Why "must"?
It's no solution to invoke Real Life
or even to explain the continuous *act*
of form by fairly sweeping everything

under the threadbare rug of Genius
or Heredity, Compensation, or Disease.
No, these are nothing but the fairy tales
we tell each other to find some comfort
for knowing nothing but the words . . .
The Master's life of words—so different from
the life I'm living now, which may be why

he knows so much about it: *makes it up*,
which I can never trust myself to do.
I've given him the goods—or bads—of it,
from which he just *makes up* whatever he needs
or wants me for. Oh not my wretched books!
He hasn't had a moment's use for them,
and that doesn't seem to matter . . . to him.

Item: "Your last book has a sense of life,
but you've never made out, recognized,
and then stuck to the center of your subject—
the marital, sexual, bedroom relations of
the man and his wife, relations which must be
tackled and faced to mean anything. You don't
tackle and face them, dearest Hugh, you can't!"

By which I guess he means I can't stick to
the *m s b* relations of man and wife
because, although a man, I have no wife
and never will. Which puts me in the same
basket of crabs with Henry James himself,
who's made those damn relations one of his
sovereign themes, however queerly phrased,

however qualified. That's right: *he* makes it up,
all of it, and *I*—I put down words I know
because I've heard them, like poor prying Bert
listening at the door to the box (and to
the stage beyond) but not a syllable
the wiser for it. Somehow the Master knows
because he *doesn't* know. Knows everything.

Tonight, I thought, both host and guest
were in the dark, but in the dark is where
the Master claims he does his work, and where
he finds his light. I suppose—I *know*—
he doesn't care (as Mrs. Wharton cares)
for the Prix Nobel—she's never met a prize
she didn't want, even for someone else . . .

And the bad thing, or the sad thing is
I'm just like her, but not so generous.
Unlike us, the Master can accept no sphere
of life (even glorification) in exchange
for life itself. For him there is no escape
from the bondage of his form of speech,
so he has no patience with a public (though

I think he longs for one). And he does have me . . .
It will be *my* generosity, this reverence
I have for every scrap of what he writes.
Not even Mrs. Wharton can say that—
she missed the allusion to our Belgian friend
in *The Wings of the Dove*. How much else?
It is a known fact that most of us resent

demands for total attention and response—
we like to have our great men, but we like
to keep their greatness on the side, without
our seeming to notice it, without pain.
The Master inflicts continual pain, which I
continually endure. Whether or not
he knows, or cares to know, I'll never tell

how Edith Wharton and the rest of us
tried and failed to obtain that prize for him,
and that will be my own revenge for pain.
He'll never know I've taken it, which is
the only victory over him I care to win.
Albeit shardless, shredless, Bertless,
he is the greatest man I've ever known.